T0020754

MY FIRST
Ballet Class

By Alyssa Satin Capucilli
Photographs by Leyah Jensen

Ready-to-Read

Simon Spotlight
New York   London   Toronto   Sydney   New Delhi
This book was previously published with slightly different text and art.

To dance lovers, everywhere!
— A.S.C.

For Mimi, still pirouetting in her handmade shoes!
— L.J.

SIMON SPOTLIGHT
An imprint of Simon & Schuster Children's Publishing Division
1230 Avenue of the Americas, New York, New York 10020
This Simon Spotlight edition December 2016
Text copyright © 2011 by Alyssa Satin Capucilli
All photographs of the boy ballet dancer copyright © 2016 by Thinkstock
All other photographs and illustrations copyright © 2011 by Simon & Schuster, Inc.
All rights reserved, including the right of reproduction in whole or in part in any form.
SIMON SPOTLIGHT, READY-TO-READ, and colophon are registered trademarks of Simon & Schuster, Inc.
For information about special discounts for bulk purchases, please contact Simon & Schuster Special Sales at
1-866-506-1949 or business@simonandschuster.com.
Manufactured in the United States of America 1116 LAK
2 4 6 8 10 9 7 5 3 1
This book has been cataloged with the Library of Congress.
ISBN 978-1-4814-7935-6 (hc)
ISBN 978-1-4814-7934-9 (pbk)
ISBN 978-1-4814-7936-3 (eBook)
This book was previously published with slightly different text and art.

It is my very first
ballet class.
I am ready to go!

I have a leotard, tights, and new slippers, too.

I wonder what we will do!

We warm up our bodies
so we are ready to dance.

Miss Lavender says, "Stretch up high!"

Then she tells us to
reach for a star!

I can do it!

I can reach up far!

We stand at the barre
and bend our knees.

In ballet that is called a plié.

I stand on my tiptoes.

I am oh so tall!

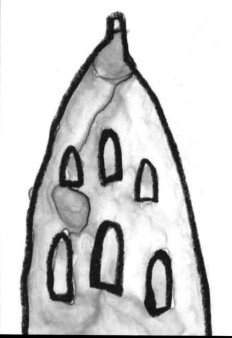

I can balance!

I do not even fall!

It is time to pretend

we are ponies now.

Off we gallop

across the room.

"Neigh! Neigh!" we say.

I jump, and I prance.

This is fun!

I do love to dance!

I point my toes.

I flutter my arms.

I bend, bow,
and sway.

I whirl and twirl
all the way home.

I cannot wait to come back to ballet!

Do you want to be a ballet dancer?

Find a grown-up to help you learn the

ballet moves in this book!

Warm up!

1 First Position

Put your feet flat on the floor.
Touch your heels together.
Pretend there's a yummy
ice-cream cone between your toes!
That's first position!

2 Second Position

Take one foot and step out to the side
just a bit. That's second position.

3
Bend and Stretch!

Bend your knees, and then . . .

stretch as high as you can!

Wiggle your fingers to the sky!

Can you catch a star?

Barre Exercises

1 Plié

Put your hands on a table or the back of a chair like it's a ballet barre. Make a piece of pizza with your feet.

Bend your knees.
Go a tiny bit down . . .
and then back up.
That is called a plié!

2 Relevé

Hold on to the table or chair.

Stretch up, up, up on your tippy-toes.

That is called a relevé!

Can you let go of the chair and balance?

Pretend there is a magic feather on your head.

Don't let it
fall off now!
Good for you!

Chassé Across the Floor!

1

Put your hands on your hips.
Point both feet straight ahead.

2

Bend your knees a bit.
Slide just one foot forward.

3

Give a tiny hop, and . . .
let the foot in back catch
up to the front.

Let's try a bit faster.
Slide, hop!
Slide, hop!
Slide, hop!

Off you go, little pony!
Chassé! Chassé!

Whirl and Twirl!

1 Lift Your Arms!

Make a big circle with your arms.

Pretend you are holding a balloon!

Can you lift it over your head?

2 Bend and Sway!

Now just bend at the waist. Stand up straight again.

Stretch up to your tippy-toes.

3 Twirl!

Step out to the side and turn your body all around.

Whirl and twirl!

Whirl and twirl!

Whee . . . ballet is fun!

4
The Big Finish!

Take a bow! Bravo!

I can't wait for my next class!